BEST OF
RESTAURANT DESIGN

Imprint
The Deutsche Bibliothek is registering this publication in the Deutsche Nationalbibliographie; detailed bibliographical information can be found on the internet at http://dnb.ddb.de

ISBN 978-3-938780-69-5
© 2009 by Verlagshaus Braun
www.verlagshaus-braun.de

1st edition 2009

Editorial staff: Annika Schulz
Translation: Stephen Roche, Hamburg
Graphic concept: Michaela Prinz

BEST OF
RESTAURANT DESIGN

Preface

This volume brings together 42 exclusively designed restaurants, whose guests are assured not only epicurean delights, but satisfaction for all the senses. Indeed, France's first great restaurateur, Antoine Beauvilliers, who opened his Grande Taverne de Londres in Paris in 1782 and later revealed his secrets in the volume L' Art du cuisinier (which remains a standard reference work on haute cuisine), emphasized the importance of not only serving food and drink in the correct order, but also of creating the right spatial environment for fine dining. One of Beauvilliers' most frequent patrons was the famous gastronome Jean-Anthelme Brillat-Savarin. In his book, The Physiology of Taste, this early restaurant critic confirmed that the Grande Taverne de Londres successfully united the key requirements of fine dining: an elegant setting, friendly service, a well-maintained wine cellar and outstanding cuisine. Brillat-Savarin deliberately mentioned the elegant surroundings first.

The restaurants featured in this book represent a global smorgasbord of interior design possibilities. They are located in cities as far apart as New York, London, Melbourne, Shanghai, Paris or Berlin, to name but a few of the cities represented. No less varied than the menus are the design concepts that have shaped these spaces. In recent years restaurants have found themselves competing with the new domestic dining room, which has arrived in many private residences due to the space-creating fusion of dining room and kitchen. These new living and eating spaces increasingly act as venues for

This **design plays** with the **old** and **the new**

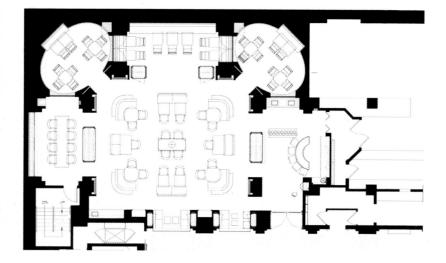

Azul + Café Sambal l Miami l Tony Chi and Associates

This **design** uses **dark wood, white marble** surfaces and seats of **woven rawhide**

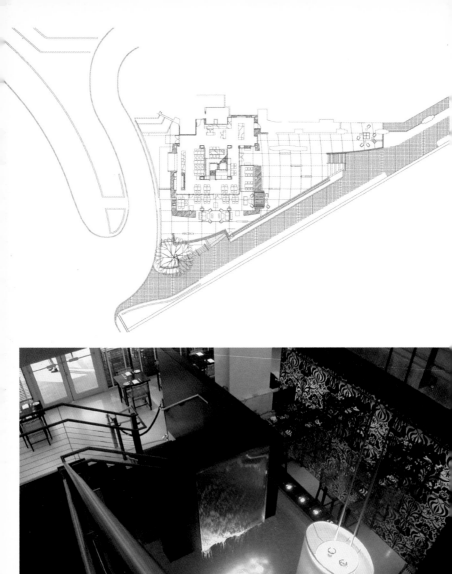

Beef Club | Wolfsburg | Stephen Williams Architects

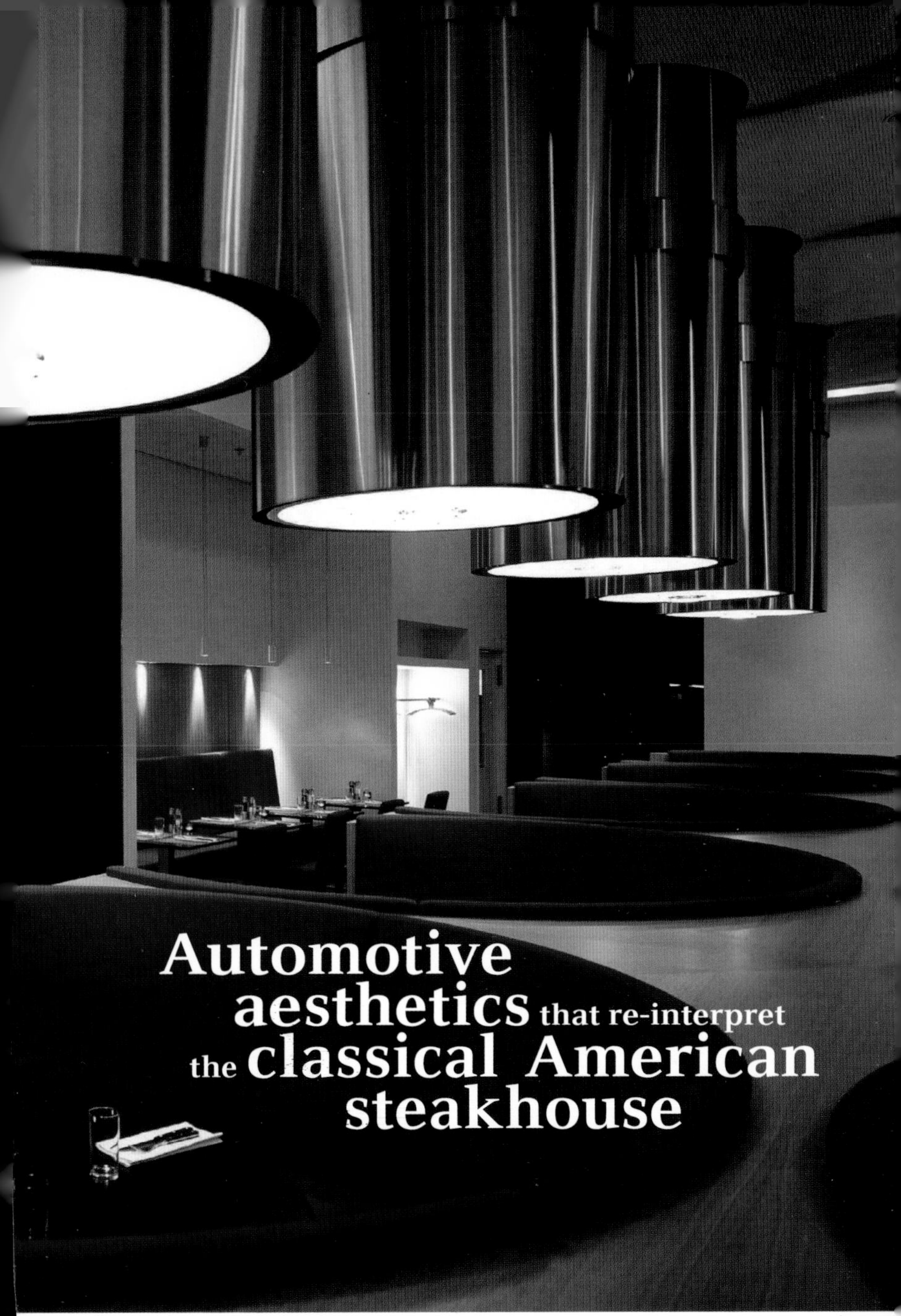

Automotive **aesthetics** that re-interpret the **classical American steakhouse**

Furnishing and materials create a homelike sitting-room with an informal atmosphere

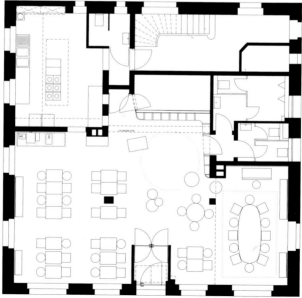

Old and new elements
in a multi-level setting

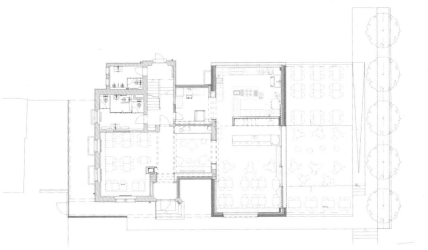

Buson Buffett | Haeundae-gu Busan | Studio Gaia

Dining booths are distributed **throughout** the restaurant to **break up** the symmetry and monotony **of the space**

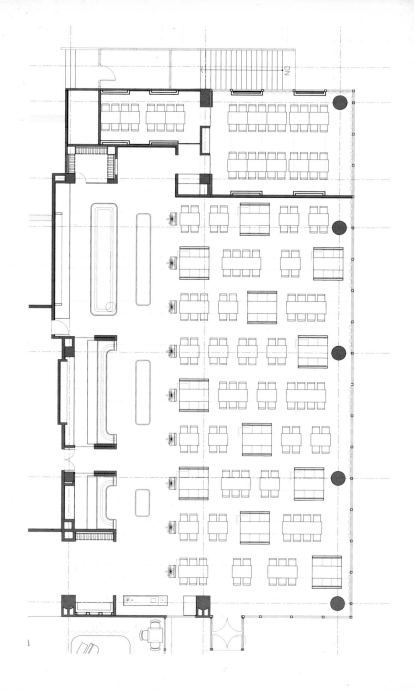

Canteen | London | Universal Design Studio

CANTEEN

Modern **British food** is reflected
in **interior materials** and a
spatial reference to **democratic**
dining spaces

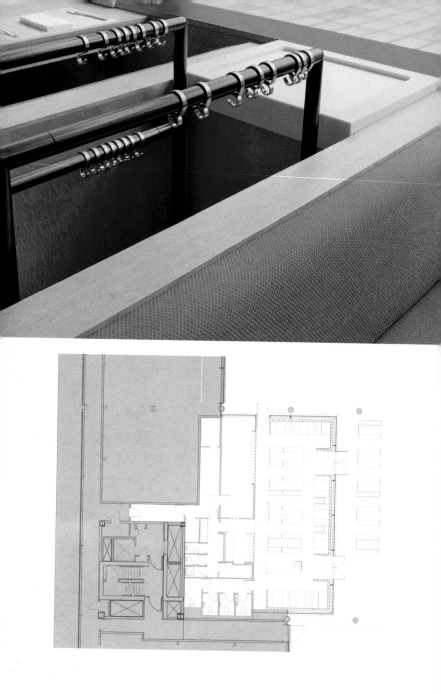

Colorful **floral patterns** and **translucent curtains** create a modern **atmosphere**

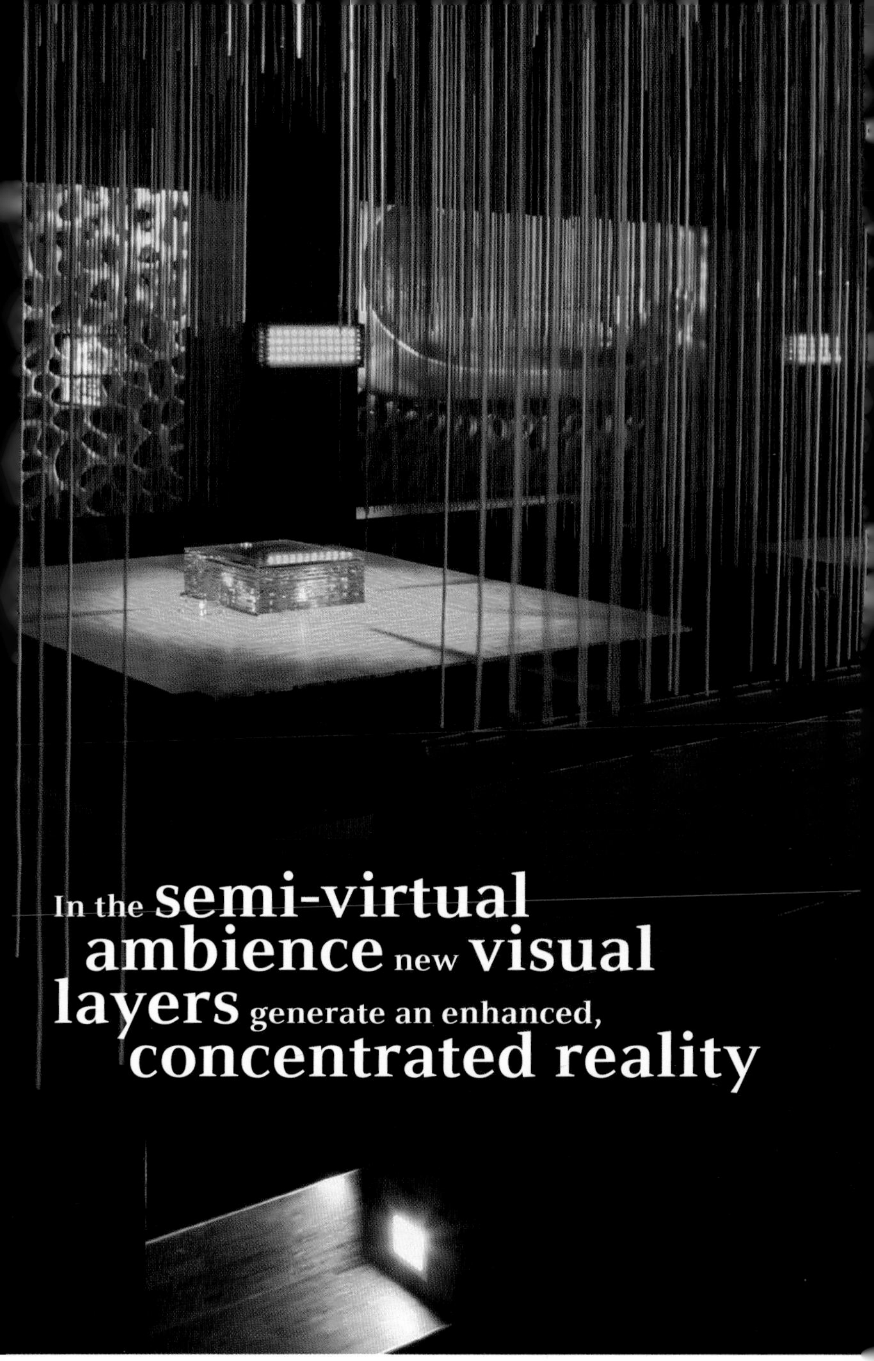

In the **semi-virtual ambience** new **visual layers** generate an enhanced, **concentrated reality**

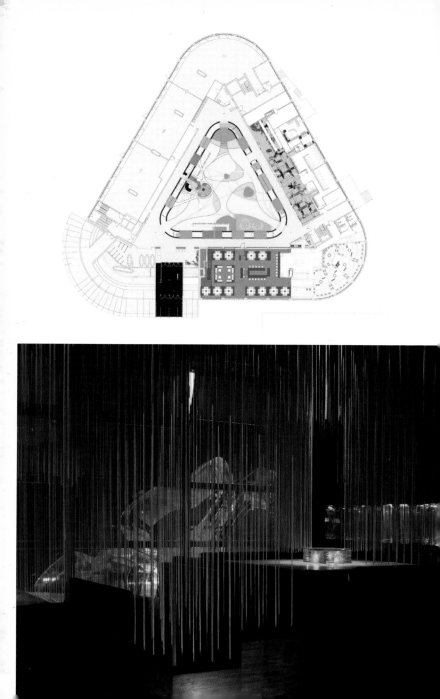

A simple yet **rich interior**
with a limited palette of
bronze, walnut, steel,
and **leather**

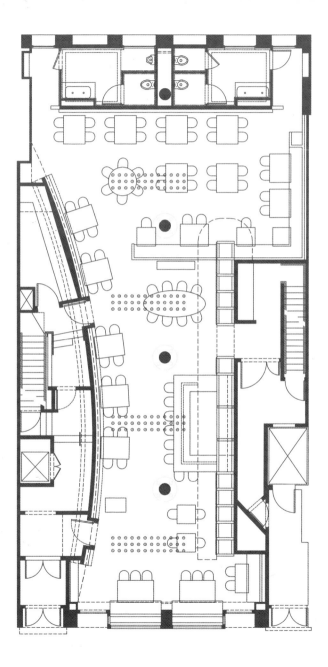

Danbo Fun | Shanghai | MoHen Design International | Hank M. Chao

The **vinyl floor** tile with **optical arts** patterns reinforce the **visual impact** of the **yolk**

Basic essentials
like the **chandelier**
make this **place special**

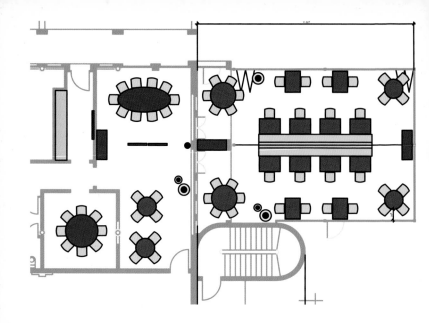

Designed to create an elegant yet casual dining experience, inspired by the cuisine

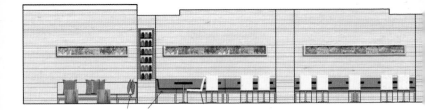

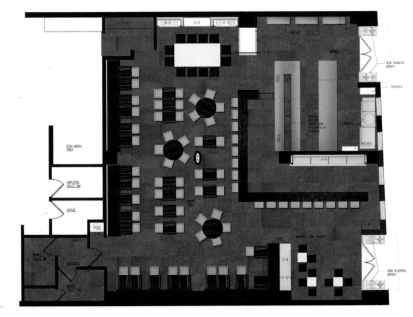

Birch logs act both as **opaque** room divider and **symbols** of natures

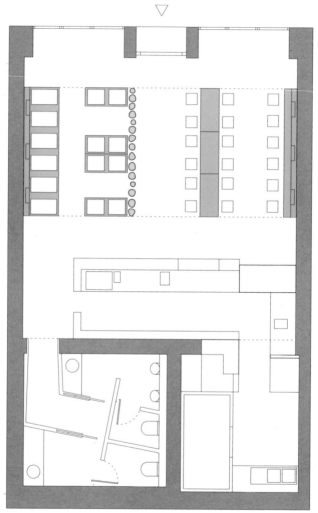

This is **where**
lifestyle comes **to life**

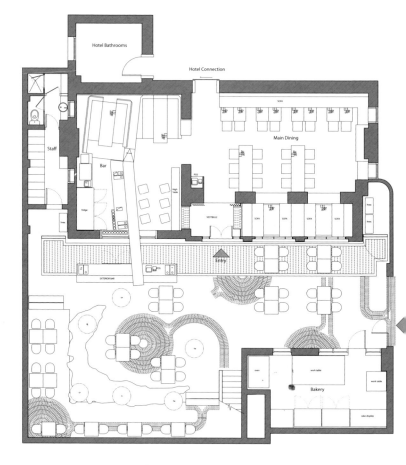

Hotel Bathrooms

Hotel Connection

SOFA

Main Dining

Staff

Bar

POS

High
table

VESTIBULE

SOFA SOFA SOFA SOFA

fridge

Entry

EXTERIOR BAR

Bakery

oven work table

work table

cake display

A **clear** and **open interior** that shifts the **focus** to the culinary art

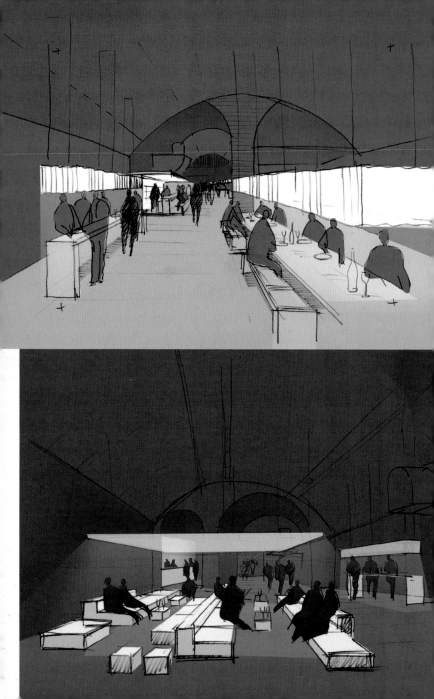

Sliding doors divide the classical and modern dining zones

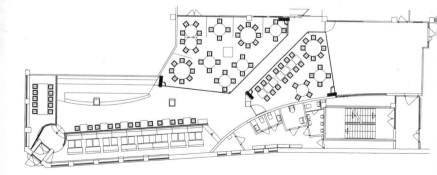

Georges | Paris | Jakob + MacFarlane

Creating a **new landscape** **camouflaged** interiors and **exteriors**

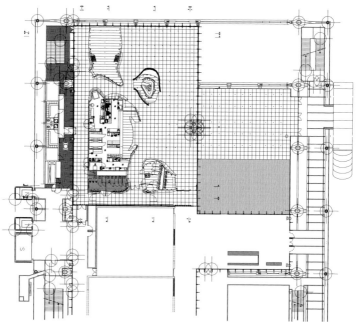

The **design draws** on traditional **Asian materials** with **walls** lined of **dark bamboo** poles

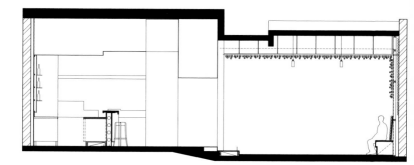

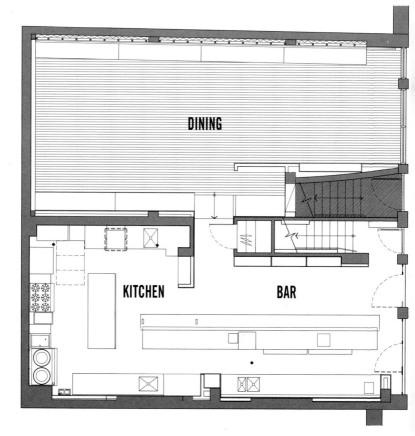

DINING

KITCHEN

BAR

An **earth palette** of **fabrics** and **furniture** grounds the **restaurant**

This restaurant offers **culinary delights** in an **open space** with a **unique lighting installation**

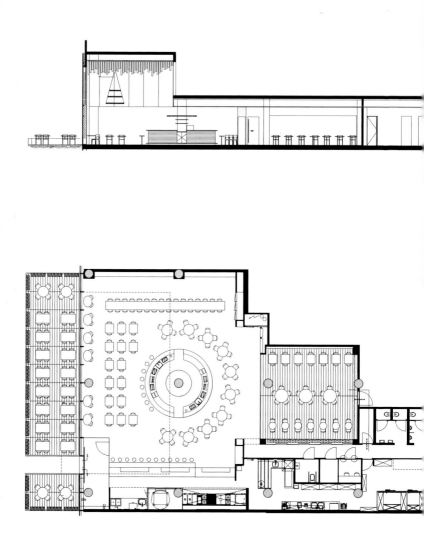

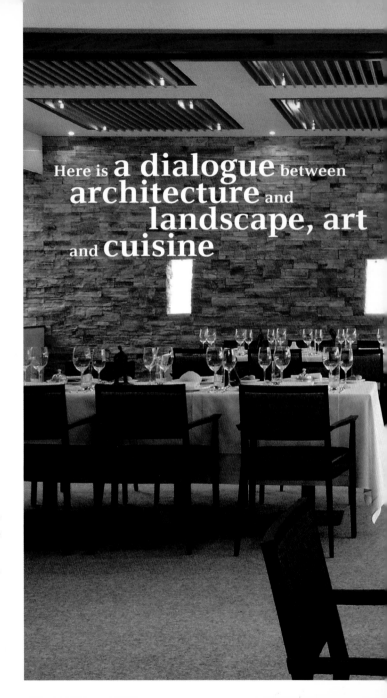

Here is **a dialogue** between **architecture** and **landscape, art** and **cuisine**

Long, extended, **plain tables** dominate the **central** dining zone

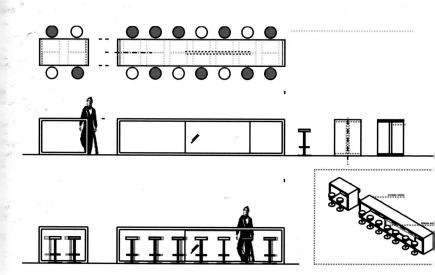

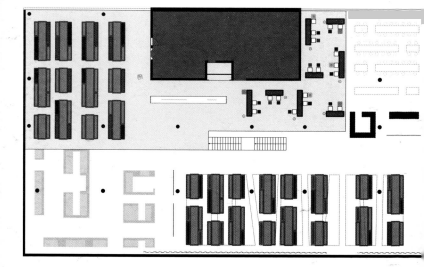

230 | **Isola Bar & Grill** | Hong Kong | Leigh & Orange

Pine floors from London and the white furnishings create a sun-bathed setting

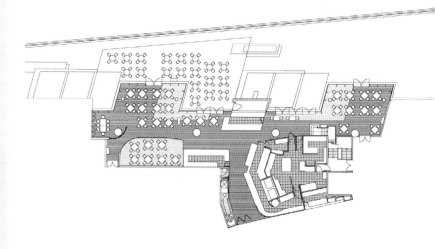

Kosushi Daslu | São Paulo | Arthur Casas Arquitetura e Design

Enjoy the **interaction** between the **solid** and **irregula** wood table, and **Tuca Reinés'** **photos**

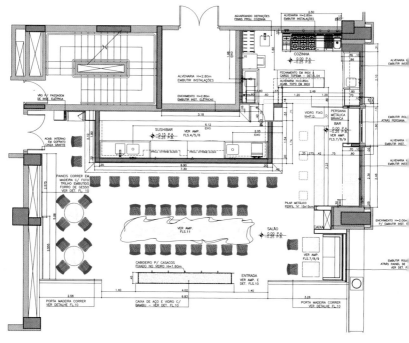

PLANTA LAYOUT
KOSUSHI DASLU
ESCALA 1:50

Lucky Devils | Los Angeles | John Friedman Alice Kimm Architects

The **wall-length photographic image** of Highway 101 **creates** a distinct L.A. vibe

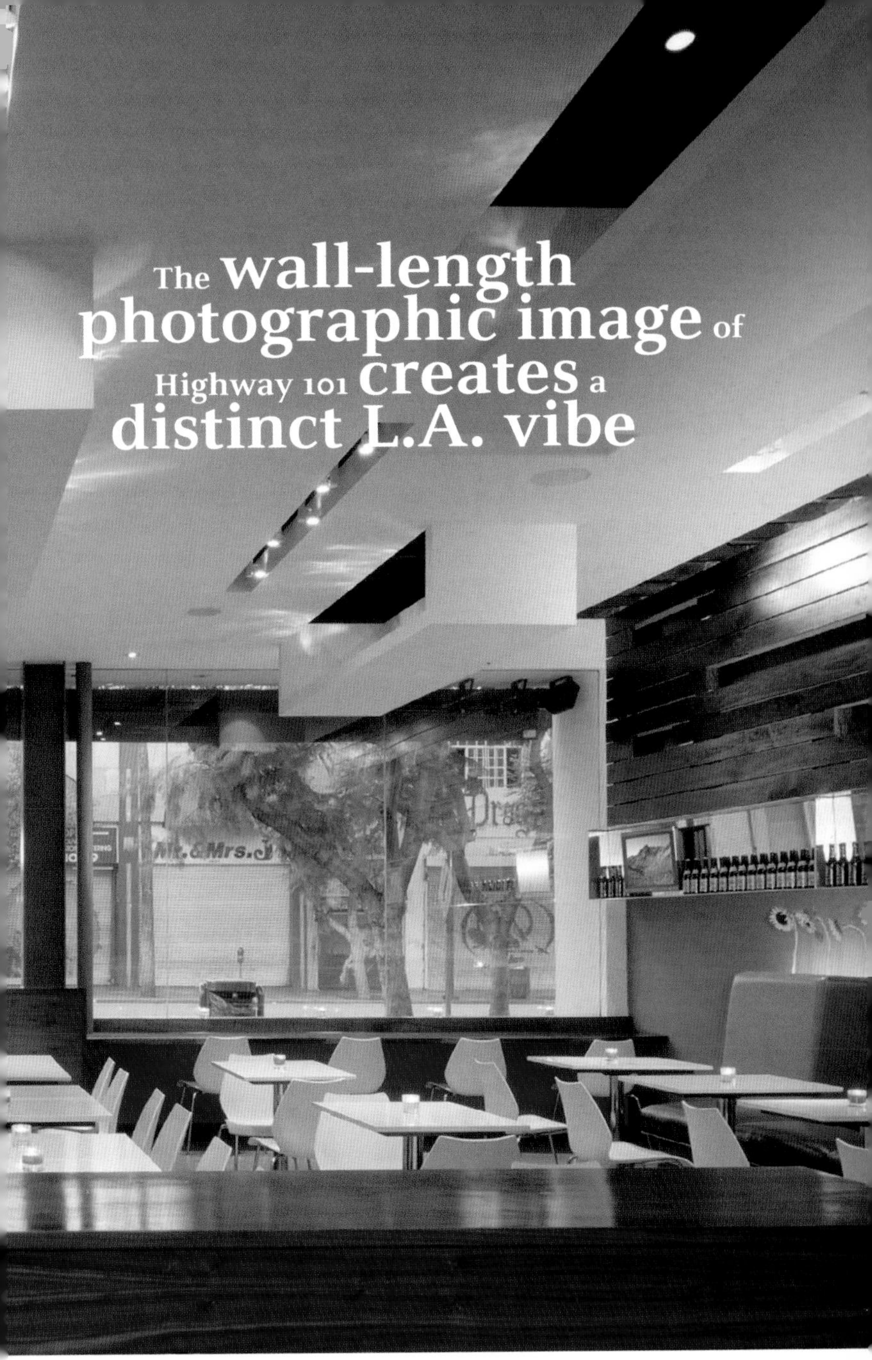

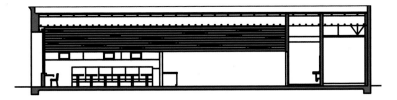

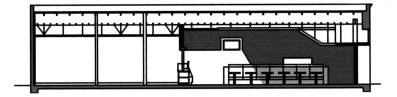

Morimoto | Philadelphia | Karim Rashid Inc.

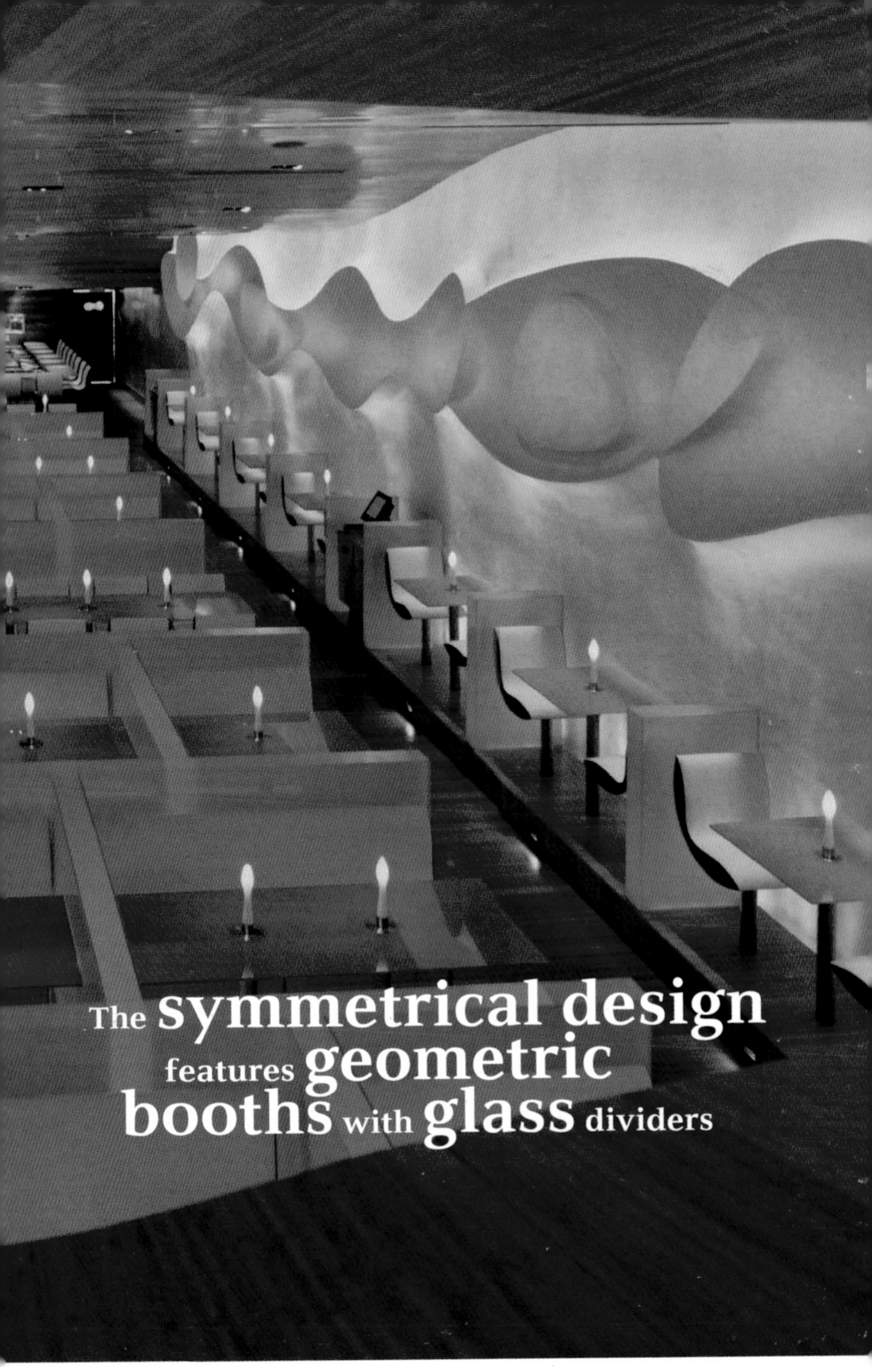

The **symmetrical design** features **geometric** **booths** with **glass** dividers

Filly   Restaurant Philly

Kitchen

Lift floor

wall

A **solid oak bar** forms the **heart** of this **establishment**

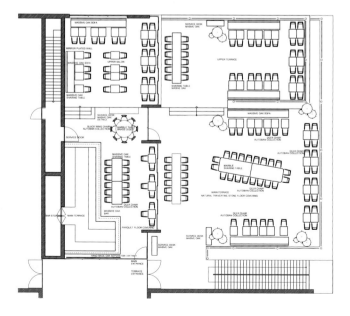

One-stop **urban-chic** experience of **wining, dining** and **dancing**

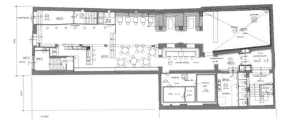

An aquarium of delights, this space references the ocean throughout

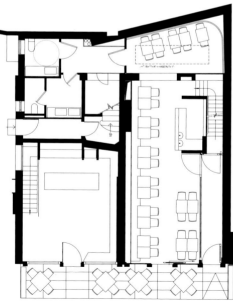

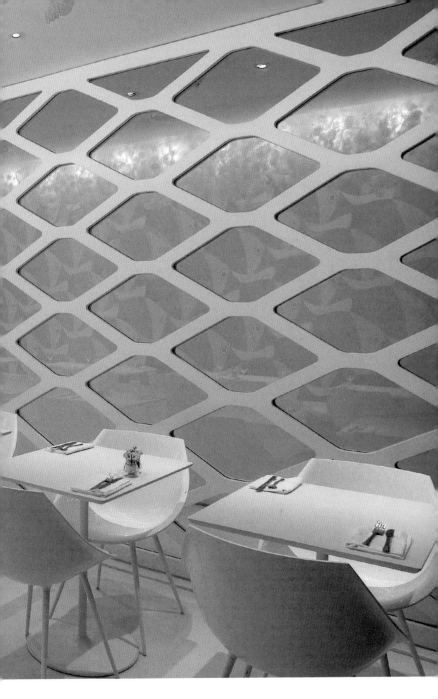

This design makes a **very clear, bold** and **graphic statement**

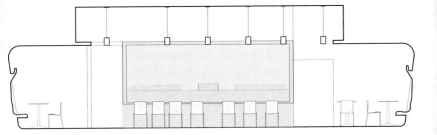

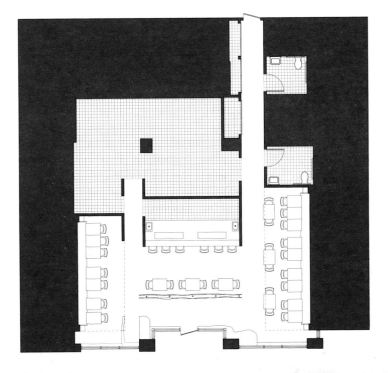

An **unaffected use** of
materials, with **little attention**
to **trendy** design

Brass, oak and
strong colors create
a **relaxing** atmosphere

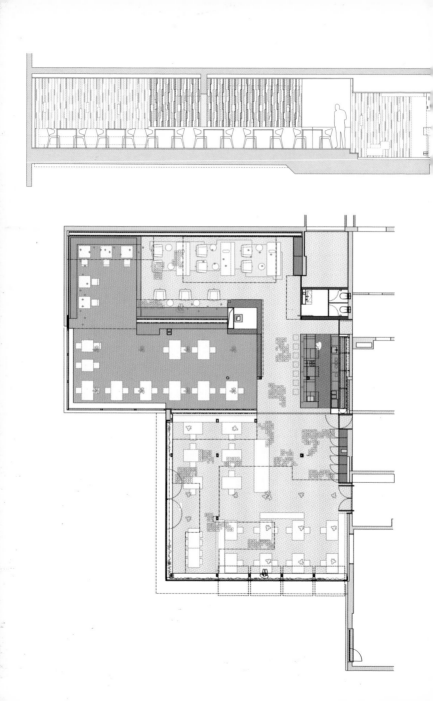

A distinguished **atmosphere** is created by **strong colors** and **unique** materials

Pommes Boutique | Munich | T. Unterlandstättner M. Schmöller Architects

LE

7

1,90
1,90
1,90

LD / GREEN LEMON / ALK FREI   2,50

ECCO   IN DER DOSE

RBLÜTE / VANILLE   4,50

WEIN

NAY / MERLOT   5,90

HEISSER

LÜHWEIN

AVERNA   2

PIRCHER WILL   2

LONGDRINKS   < 3

GIN TONIC / CUBA LIBRE / VODKA BULL 5,90

FLASCHE MARY JANE VODKA

...KS
PILS / GOLD / GREEN LEMON / ALK.FREI   2,50

...RL SECCO   IN DER DOSE
HOLUNDERBLÜTE / VANILLE   4,50

...AFFE WEIN
CHARDONNAY / MERLOT   5,90

HEISSER ZIMT-APFELSAFT
TASSE GLÜHWEIN
AVERNA
PIRCHER WILLIAMS
LONGDRINKS
   GIN TONIC / CUBA LIBRE / VODKA BULL

FLASCHE MARY JANE VODKA 0,2l

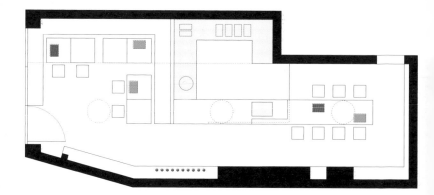

Glossy red furniture
stands out against
a lush green floor

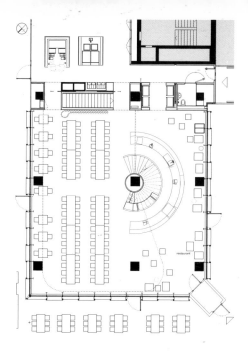

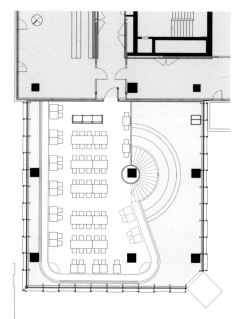

Readily available materials transform a slot space into a restaurant

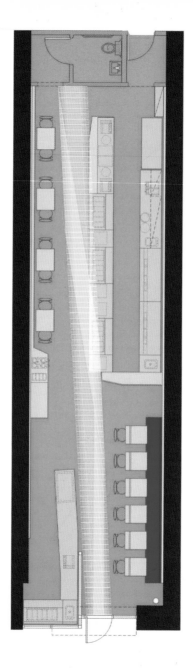

346 | **Schneeweiß** | Berlin | unit-berlin, architecture and media design

White materials and furniture combine to produce an enchanting effect

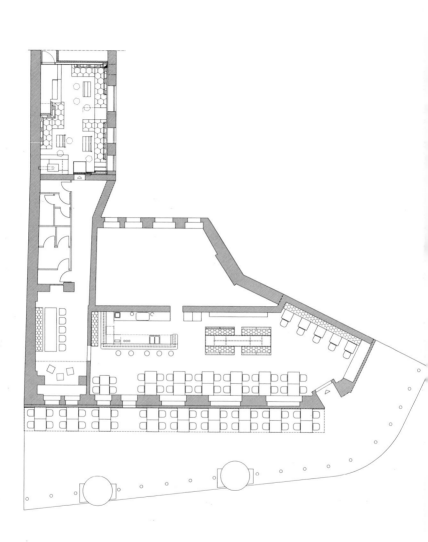

356 | **Slanted Door** | San Francisco | Lundberg Design

Architectural design that presents **natural elements** in an **inventive** and **simple manner**

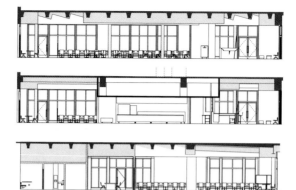

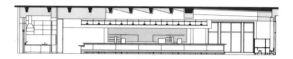

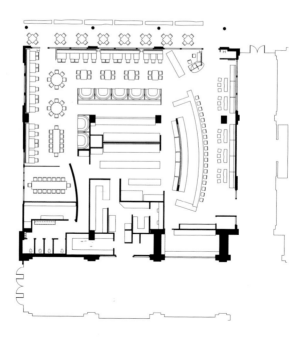

The **bourbon-toned wood, raw steel** and **cork** demonstrate a **natural elegance**

Warm colors and
harmonic proportions
give this restaurant a
perfect sense of space

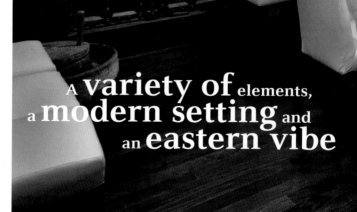

A **variety of** elements, a **modern setting** and an **eastern vibe**

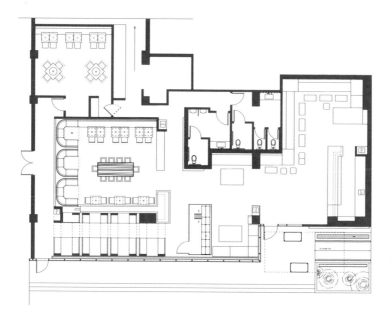

VAU l Berlin l gmp Architekten – von Gerkan, Marg und Partner

The **design** is characterized **by a combination** of **glass** and **steel, slate** and **pearwood**

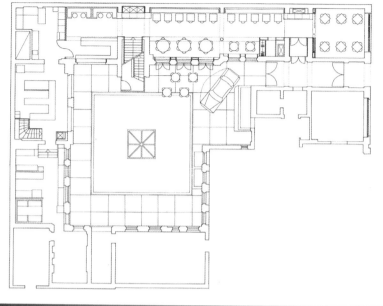

Architects Index

Picture Credits